...NED STATIONS ON LONDON'S UNDERGROUND

A Photographic Record

J.E. CONNOR

Preface

This book is a companion to my previous volume *London's Disused Underground Stations*, and provides a photographic record of many stations which are no longer open. Brief historical data is included, however readers who require further information are recommended to consult the earlier publication, which is a detailed study of all abandoned LUL stations within the London Boroughs.

Each route has been dealt with alphabetically, with stations appearing in geographical order. I have used current line titles to assist the reader in identifying present day remains, although some historical anomalies have occurred. Of particular note is the route to Hounslow, which was worked from the outset by the Metropolitan District Railway, and continued to be part of the District Line until 1964. As it is now only served by the Piccadilly Line, it appears under that heading. This means that the short branch to Hounslow Town, closed in 1909, would be completely isolated if correctly shown as 'District', so it is featured in the Piccadilly section.

The book is intended to be largely pictorial. Therefore I have ensured that, except for the odd unavoidable case, there has been no duplication of photographs with the previous volume. I have also included sections of line outside the bounds of Greater London, such as the Brill branch, together with routes associated with London Transport but not actually part of the Underground system. These include the Docklands Light Railway, and the station at Uxbridge Road, which until 1940 was served by Metropolitan trains linking Edgware Road with Earl's Court.

I have featured stations which have been totally closed, together with those where the platforms have been relocated on completely new sites. I have intentionally avoided rebuildings such as West Hampstead and Northwood, where platforms have been moved laterally in connection with track alterations, and also instances of street level buildings being discarded in favour of newer entrances, as at Euston and Green Park.

Photograph credits

London Transport Museum : 6, 7 (both), 8 (both), 10 (upper), 11 (upper), 17, 22, 23 (upper), 24, 25 (lower), 32, 34, 35 (both), 38, 39 (lower), 40, 45 (upper), 50, 55, 56 (both), 66, 67 (lower), 69 (lower), 72, 73 (upper), 75, 76 (upper), 77, 81, 85 (upper), 86 (upper), 87.

I. Baker : 51 (lower), 85 (centre).

A.E. Bennett : 82, 83 (upper).

H.C. Casserley : 93 (upper).

R.M. Casserley : 12.

J.E. Connor : 4 (all), 10 (lower), 18, 19 (both), 21 (lower), 26 (both), 27, 28 (both), 29 (all), 30 (all), 33, 36, 37 (both), 39 (upper), 41, 42 (both), 43, 52 (lower), 59 (upper), 60, 64, 67 (upper), 68 (lower), 69 (upper), 70 (both), 71 (both), 73 (lower), 74 (both), 78 (lower), 83 (centre and lower), 91 (both), 92 (both), 96 (centre).

J.E. Connor Collection : 11 (lower), 14, 15 (both), 16 (upper), 20, 21 (upper), 23 (lower), 25 (upper), 31, 46, 51 (upper), 52 (upper), 61 (both), 62, 65 (both), 78 (upper), 86 (lower), 89 (upper), 90 (lower), 93 (lower).

M. Durrell Collection : 45 (lower), 57 (both), 68 (upper).

G.W. Goslin Collection : 49 (both).

Lens of Sutton : 13 (both), 16 (lower), 48 (both), 53, 76 (lower), 80, 85 (lower).

Photomatic : 89 (lower), 90 (upper).

D. Rose : 59 (lower).

Southern Railway : 84.

Line engravings from contemporary publications etc : 54, 95, 96.

ISBN 0 947699 30 9
Published by Connor & Butler Ltd.,
69 Guildford Road, Colchester, Essex.
Printed by Juniper House of Print.
© Connor & Butler Ltd. 2000.

Contents

Maps

Index

All stations are included under the names which they carried at time of closure. These are shown in this index in capital letters, whilst alternative names appear in upper and lower case. Those shown within quotation marks and italicised were proposed but never carried. Stations which appear in bold type are illustrated.

Introduction

The closed stations on London's Underground are many and varied. Some lie hidden away behind walls on deep level tube lines, whilst others can be easily seen. As the years progress, a number have passed beyond living memory, and it may be hard to imagine that each of them was once a familiar feature to past generations of Londoners.

Occasionally it is possible to glimpse these old stations from passing trains, although it takes a very experienced eye to recognise some of them. Nevertheless, a few remain obvious, and the imaginative traveller can easily conjure up thoughts of ghosts lurking in the dark cross passages.

It is perhaps this air of mystery which adds to their interest. After all, there are numerous disused station sites on the main line suburban routes around London, but somehow, these do not seem to exude the same atmosphere as one which lies seemingly forgotten in the gloom of a tunnel.

A few abandoned Underground stations were put to good use during the Second World War, when they were converted into air raid shelters, whilst a couple on the Piccadilly Line were adapted for government purposes. Even today, ephemeral relics such as faded paper signs pointing to long gone wartime first aid posts still cling to walls, and although passed by millions of passengers daily, these remain largely unseen.

This book takes a look at the various forgotten stations on the Underground system, and tells of when they were built, why they were closed, and what, if anything, still survives of them.

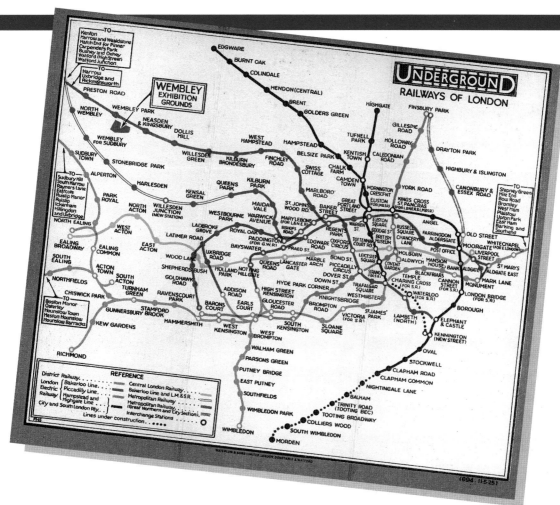

The Underground network has undergone drastic expansion and numerous changes since this map, designed by F.H. Stingemore, was published in 1924.

At this time, the Piccadilly Line only linked Hammersmith with Finsbury Park, whilst what is now the High Barnet/Mill Hill East section of the Northern Line terminated at Highgate, or Archway as the station later became.

The Central Line was restricted to the route between Liverpool Street and Ealing Broadway, whilst both the Victoria and Jubilee Lines were still very much in the future.

Stations shown on this map which have since completely closed are:

Aldwych
British Museum
Brompton Road
Down Street
Marlborough Road
St. Johns Wood Road
St. Mary's
South Acton
Swiss Cottage
Uxbridge Road
Wood Lane
York Road

Some have also been subject to resiting or renaming.

Wood Lane

In order to serve the Franco-British Exhibition, the Central London Railway decided to build a new station near its existing depot at Wood Lane. The line was extended from the former terminus at Shepherds Bush, and reached the new premises by way of a sharply-curved single track loop.

The station was brought into use on 14th May 1908, to coincide with the opening of the exhibition, and had its entrance on the east side of Wood Lane.

The street level building was designed by Harry Bell Measures, and stood partly beneath an ornate overhead walkway which linked the exhibition grounds with Uxbridge Road. In this view, the CLR power station, with the word 'Tube' displayed on its chimney can be seen in the background.

On arrival at Wood Lane, passengers originally alighted at platform one, which is seen to the left, then made their way to the exhibition by means of the footbridge. Those travelling towards central London joined their train from platform two, on which the photographer was standing when this view was taken in 1935.

When the Central London Line was extended to Ealing Broadway in 1920, two sub-surface platforms were added to Wood Lane. Because the station still had to be reached by way of the old single track loop however, it was not ideal, so eventually replacement premises were opened at White City on 23rd November 1947, and Wood Lane was closed. The platform seen here is still visible from passing eastbound trains.

An idiosyncracy of Wood Lane station was this section of moveable platform, added to the east end of No 1 in 1928. Its existence allowed longer trains to be operated, as when the depot needed to be accessed, it could be swung clear of the points by the signal man in the adjoining cabin.

British Museum

British Museum station was opened by the Central London Railway on 30th July 1900, and had its entrance at the corner of High Holborn and Bloomsbury Court.

After the opening of the nearby Great Northern Piccadilly & Brompton Railway station at Holborn, passengers began using this as an interchange with British Museum, but the facilities were less than perfect, and meant walking between the two at street level.

A plan to build new Central London Line platforms at Holborn was authorised in 1914, but the scheme failed to materialise due to the intervention of the First World War.

It was later revived however, and the new station was brought into use on 25th September 1933, when British Museum closed.

Soon after the CLR opened, Shurrey's Publications issued a series of postcards featuring cartoon characters at each of the stations. Generally the names were shown correctly, but in the case of British Museum, an abbreviated form was used, presumably for humorous reasons!

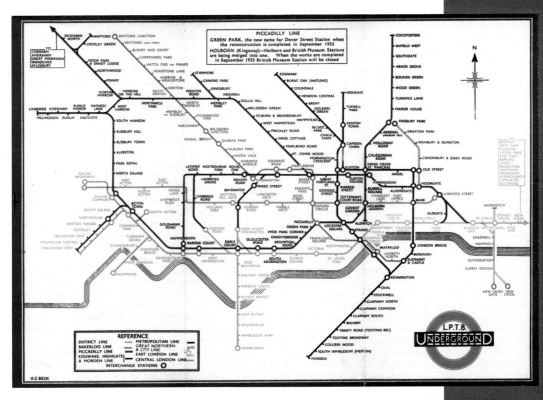

The eastbound side at British Museum soon after opening, showing the white tiled walls, and wooden platforms which were featured at all original CLR stations. The latter became regarded as a potential fire hazard, and were therefore rebuilt in concrete, with those at British Museum being replaced towards the end of 1909.

The street level building, designed by Harry Bell Measures, as it appeared in 1989, shortly before demolition. It was originally constructed with a flat roof, but this was only intended as a temporary arrangement, as office accommodation was erected above it around 1902.

During the Second World War, the former platform tunnels were converted into air raid shelters, and these were brought into use in September 1941. The accommodation was located on two levels, with an upper floor being specially constructed from concrete. Here workmen are standing on this floor as they build a wall to separate the shelter facilities from passing trains on 19th June 1941.

All that now survives are the grimy white tiled walls at track level, which can still be seen from a passing train.

Epping-Ongar

The line linking Loughton and Epping with Ongar was opened by the Great Eastern Railway on 24th April 1865.

Under a pre-Second World War plan, the Central Line was to extend eastwards from its existing terminus at Liverpool Street, and ultimately travel through to Ongar. The branch first appeared on Underground maps in 1938, but work was delayed by the outbreak of hostilities the following year, and the route was not officially absorbed by London Transport until 25th September 1949.

In the meantime, tube services were extended to Woodford in 1947, and eventually reached Epping two years later. However, the remainder of the branch was destined to retain a shuttle service of steam trains until 18th November 1957, when electrification to Ongar was finally completed.

Unfortunately, the single track section between Epping and Ongar served a lightly populated area, and by 1970 was losing around £100,000 a year. This led to it being proposed for closure, but although the branch survived, its existence remained under threat, and services subsequently became restricted to peak hours only.

Eventually, the inevitable happened, and closure came after traffic on Friday 30th September 1994.

There have been proposals to reopen it as a private railway, but by the end of 1999 it still remained out of use.

The first station beyond Epping was North Weald, where a passing loop was brought into use on 14th August 1949. The expected increase in traffic never materialised however, so this was closed from 17th October 1976. In this view, ex-GER Class F5 2-4-2T No 67200 is seen working the branch push-pull service on 16th April 1957.

Blake Hall had the unenviable reputation of being the least used station on the LT system, and closed after traffic on 31st October 1981. Here it is seen in LNER days, with its goods yard which remained in use until 18th April 1966, and the signal box, just visible behind a tree on the left, which lasted until 1949.

The terminus at Ongar comprised a single platform, and in steam days boasted a single-road engine shed of 1865 vintage. Freight traffic was handled in the station goods yard until 18th April 1966, and the signal box was abolished three years later.

South Acton

On 15th May 1899, a 1,232 yard single line spur was opened for freight traffic between the Metropolitan District Railway at Mill Hill Park (now Acton Town) and South Acton on the North & South Western Junction Railway.

Six years later the track was doubled, and electrified. A single platform station was constructed at South Acton, and a passenger service commenced on 13th June 1905.

At first, passenger trains operated between South Acton and Hounslow Barracks, but in time destinations also included South Harrow and Uxbridge.

The line joined the NSWJR at District Junction, a little beyond South Acton station, but the connection was only intended for freight traffic. When this ceased, the junction was no longer required, so it was severed in 1930, and two years later the second track was lifted.

From 15th February 1932, through workings from other parts of the MDR were withdrawn, and the South Acton branch was reduced to a shuttle which ran back and forth to a bay platform at Acton Town.

The MDR terminus adjoined the up side of South Acton station on the North & South Western Junction Railway (now part of the North London Line) and its entrance is seen here around 1950.

In the late 1930s, a pair of 1923 G Stock cars were converted so that they could be driven from either end. In this form they became resident on the Acton Town - South Acton shuttle, and can be seen here at the branch terminus in the 1950s.

Throughout much of the day, the service operated at ten minute intervals, and the journey time was so quick that it was thought the crew could do an out and back trip from Acton Town by the time the messroom kettle boiled. This gave rise to the turn being known by staff as 'The Tea Run', although the origin of its other nickname, 'The Pony', is rather more obscure.

Eventually however, LT announced that this unremunerative, if characterful service would cease, and trains were withdrawn after traffic on 28th February 1959. Official closure followed on 2nd March.

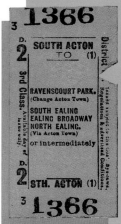

The track was lifted within a few months of closure, leaving the abandoned station to stand for a short while before it was completely demolished.

SOUTH ACTON UNDERGROUND BRANCH LINE IS NOW CLOSED

The bridge which took the branch over Bollo Lane survived a little longer, but was finally removed in January 1964. During demolition, it collapsed into the road, and traffic had to be diverted for several days whilst it was cut up on the spot.

Earl's Court

Although the street level building at the first station was modest, the same cannot be said of its 1878 replacement as seen here. This remained in its original form until 1906, when it was rebuilt as an interchange with the Great Northern Piccadilly & Brompton Railway.

The original station of this name stood on the east side of Earl's Court Road, and consisted of two platforms, one of which was an island.

Initially there was little local development, as the surrounding area was largely given over to market gardening. Therefore, the station only required to be a very modest affair, with a wooden street level building.

This was destroyed by fire on 30th December 1875, and although subsequently repaired, the decision was made to resite the premises to the opposite side of Earl's Court Road.

The replacement station opened on 1st February 1878, when its predecessor was closed, and soon demolished.

Tower Hill

The original Tower Hill station was opened as Mark Lane on 6th October 1884, and had its entrance at the corner of Byward Street and Seething Lane.

Its street level building was replaced by a new booking hall incorporated into an office block in 1911, but apart from this, the station's only major change came on 1st September 1946, when it was renamed Tower Hill.

In time, the station proved to be inadequate, and as there was no room for expansion on its existing site, authority was received to relocate the premises further east.

The site chosen was that previously occupied by the short lived Metropolitan Railway station at Tower of London *(See pp 20-21)*, and the building contract was let in November 1964.

The present Tower Hill station opened on 5th February 1967, as a direct replacement for its predecessor which closed the same day.

The westbound platform, as it appeared on 28th March 1966.

The seemingly deserted eastbound platform at Tower Hill in February 1967, shortly before the station was closed. Although the westbound side was subsequently demolished to facilitate track alterations, the platform seen here still exists, and can be glimpsed from a passing train, immediately west of the present Tower Hill.

A 1966 view of the street level entrance, as incorporated into an office block fifty-five years earlier. The lettering above the arched opening to the right read 'Mark Lane Station Chambers', but although the building still survives, this has long-since disappeared.

The Tower of London

This short lived station owed its origins to inter-company squabbling between the Metropolitan and Metropolitan District Railways regarding the completion of the Inner Circle, or Circle Line as it is now known.

The project was a joint venture between the two, but having suffered from lack of finance, the MDR section got as far east as Mansion House then stopped.

The Metropolitan however wanted to press on, and eventually built as much of the route as the authorising Parliamentary Act allowed. They finally reached Trinity Square, and on 25th September 1882 opened a station there which was named The Tower of London.

This 'go it alone' venture engendered more bad feeling between the companies, but eventually the atmosphere improved, and the Inner Circle at last became a reality.

A new station was opened at nearby Mark Lane *(See pp18-19)* on 6th October 1884, and a week later, on 13th October, The Tower of London closed.

The station was erected in the remarkably short time of two days and three nights, and was therefore a fairly simple structure. Its street level building stood on the east side of Trinity Square, near the corner with Trinity Place, and is seen here around 1901.

The disused Tower of London station remained largely intact until 1903 when its platforms were removed in connection with electrification work which was then taking place. The street level building survived much longer however, and was not demolished until September 1940, around a month after this photograph was taken. The gaps beside the line where the platforms had been removed remained visible into the 1960s, as did a short section of erstwhile stairway handrail, but with the plan to re-use the site for a new Tower Hill station, all relics of the original premises were swept away.

The contract for building the new Tower Hill station was let to W & C French Ltd in November 1964, and the new premises were brought into use, albeit in an unfinished state on 5th February 1967. Today, millions of passengers use the present Tower Hill without realising that at one time, a station called The Tower of London once stood on the same site, even if its useful life was restricted to just two years!

Aldgate East

To the west of the present Aldgate East lies the site of the first station to carry this name.

It was opened by the Metropolitan and Metropolitan District Railways on 6th October 1884, and stood on the north side of Whitechapel High Street.

So that longer trains could be accommodated between the junctions west of the station, a resiting scheme was devised.

The work of building the new station was carried out with only a minimum disruption to traffic, and the new premises were brought into use on 31st October 1938, the same day that the original closed.

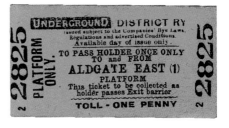

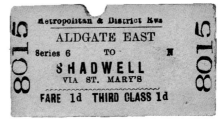

The street level building, as reconstructed under the direction of Harry Wharton Ford in 1914.

The realigned junction at Aldgate East would occupy part of the original station site, so the platforms were rebuilt in wood to make them easier to remove when the time came. The resiting project was a major engineering feat, but the only time the line needed to close was on the day of the changeover. This view shows the old station on its last night, as passengers await the final trains. The new premises were opened on 31st October 1938.

The gates leading into Harry Wharton Ford's 1914 street level building were locked, and a large sign erected on them to direct passengers to its replacement. The old building survived in a derelict condition until the 1950s when it was demolished for redevelopment.

St. Mary's (Whitechapel Rd.)

St. Mary's (Whitechapel) station opened on 3rd March 1884, and was used initially by South Eastern Railway trains from Addiscombe Road, which travelled by way of a spur off the East London Line, known as 'The St. Mary's Curve'. These were withdrawn seven months later from 1st October 1884, a week before full Metropolitan & District services were introduced over the lines east of Bishopsgate and Mansion House.

The station was renamed St. Mary's (Whitechapel Road) on 26th January 1923.

The station remained little altered throughout its existence: This is the interior of the booking hall as it appeared around 1914.

St. Mary's closed from 1st May 1938, almost six months prior to the resited Aldgate East station being opened nearby. This view shows the street level building immediately after closure, with a large board directing potential passengers to Whitechapel or Aldgate East.

In the spring of 1940, agreement was reached whereby the disused platforms could be used as air-raid shelters, but while work was under way, the street level building was badly damaged by a bomb on 22nd October 1940.
A new shelter entrance was constructed, but this was destroyed in April 1941.

The work of converting St. Mary's into a air-raid shelter continued, even though the replacement entrance was completely obliterated by bombing before it was completed. Parts of the former shelter accommodation still survives, such as this room on the old westbound platform, which is seen here in 1996.

At track level, St. Mary's remains much as it did at the end of the war in 1945, with walls close to the platform edges concealing the erstwhile shelters from passing trains. This view shows the eastbound side on 25th January 1996.

Mudchute

Until 1999, the Docklands Light Railway route which now serves Lewisham, terminated on the north bank of the Thames at Island Gardens. The final stretch of line, south of Crossharbour utilised the surviving formation of the old Millwall Extension Railway, which opened in 1871-2, and closed in 1926. Between Crossharbour and Island Gardens stood the station at Mudchute, which was located on a new section of concrete viaduct, and opened to the public with the initial section of DLR on 31st August 1987.

As it was not possible to extend the line south of the existing terminus, the route to Lewisham needed to branch off near Crossharbour, then dive into cutting, and eventually tunnel to pass under the Thames. This resulted in the earlier formation being abandoned, and the closure of the original stations at Mudchute and Island Gardens.

£0.00 ADULT 00.00   000 05421

ds   Docklands   Dockla

lands Light Railway Limited · Docklands Light Railway Limited · Do
side · See other side · See other side · See other side · See othe

THE ROYAL OPENING 30th JULY 1987 MUDCHUTE STATION

The DLR was officially opened by HM The Queen on 30th July 1987, but public services did not commence for another month. This view looks south along the platforms at Mudchute on 31st August 1987, with P86 vehicle No 08 entering en-route to Tower Gateway.

Docklands Light Railway

The last passenger trains to use the original DLR route south of Crossharbour ran on the cold, wet night of 8th/9th January 1999. Here, a train for Island Gardens arrives at Mudchute, about an hour before the station closed.

After closure, very little time elapsed before Mudchute station was demolished. On Friday 15th January 1999, the lamps and signs were removed, with the track being lifted soon after. The following week, the towers which housed the lifts were knocked down, and by the end of the month virtually everything had disappeared. The new Mudchute station is located in cutting, on a site east of its predecessor, and opened on Saturday 20th November 1999.

Island Gardens

The terminus at Island Gardens occupied part of the site once used by the former station at North Greenwich & Cubitt Town. This remained standing for forty-three years after its closure in 1926, but was eventually demolished to make way for a rowing club building. With the advent of the DLR, the rest of the site was cleared, and a new viaduct was erected to accommodate Island Gardens. Although built largely of concrete, this was faced with bricks, and the resulting arches were fitted out as shop units.

The derelict remains of North Greenwich & Cubitt Town station in 1966.

Because it used the old Millwall Extension Railway viaduct on its approach to Island Gardens, this section of the DLR was restricted to a single track. At the terminus however, it splayed out to serve two platforms, as seen here on 31st August 1987.

Island Gardens station featured a distinctive glass domed tower which accommodated lifts and a stairway, whilst the viaduct wall beneath platform 2 carried a plaque commemorating the royal opening in July 1987.

DOCKLANDS LIGHT RAILWAY
OPENED BY
HER MAJESTY THE QUEEN
30TH JULY 1987

The old Millwall Extension Railway viaduct north of the station carried the DLR above Millwall Park. This 682 yard structure was the only notable piece of civil engineering on the former MER, and although now disused for the second time in its existence, it is Grade II listed, and has been retained.

New Cross

The southern terminus of the East London Railway, which opened for public traffic from Wapping on 7th December 1869.

It comprised two platforms, and although it adjoined the eastern side of the existing London Brighton & South Coast Railway station at New Cross, it was at a slightly lower level, and completely separate.

The ELR was extended northwards to a junction with the Great Eastern Railway near Bishopsgate in April 1876, and following the introduction of through services between Liverpool Street and Croydon, the earlier terminus closed.

With the opening of the Metropolitan and Metropolitan District Joint line towards Whitechapel, both these companies began operating onto the ELR, by way of the new St. Mary's Curve, and the old New Cross terminus once again came into its own. It was reopened on 1st October 1884 for the use of MDR trains, but eventually, after track alterations had been carried out, these were diverted into the adjacent LBSCR station.

Closure came for the second time on 1st September 1886, and the abandoned terminus was eventually demolished fourteen years later.

The former LBSCR station was renamed New Cross Gate on 9th July 1923, and still serves as one of the southern termini used by today's East London Line.

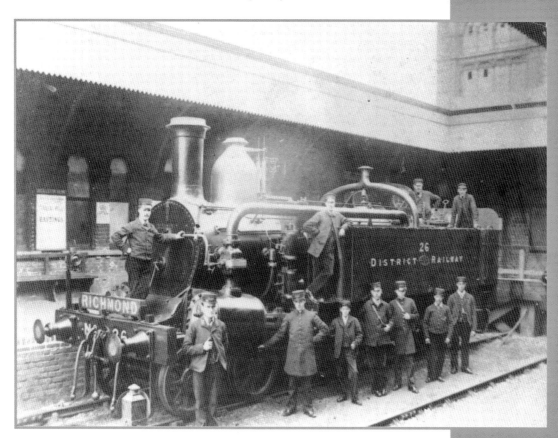

MDR 4-4-0T No 26 is seen at New Cross terminus with a line up of staff, possibly at the time of closure in 1886.

Hammersmith

The original terminus of the Hammersmith & City Railway was opened, along with the line from Bishop's Road, Paddington, on 13th June 1864. The route was independently financed, but supported by the Metropolitan and Great Western Railways. It was laid with both standard (4ft 8$\frac{1}{2}$in) and broad (7ft 0$\frac{1}{4}$in) track, as at that time the GWR still used the latter, which had been favoured by its engineer, Isambard Kingdom Brunel.

When opened, the line was served by GWR broad gauge trains which operated at half-hourly intervals between Hammersmith and Farringdon Street. At the beginning of the following month, these were joined by a GWR service which ran to Addison Road (now Kensington Olympia) via Notting Hill (now Ladbroke Grove), but it was not until 1st April 1865 that Metropolitan standard gauge trains made their debut on the route.

From 1st June 1866, the Hammersmith & City came under joint Met & GW management, and was taken over by the two larger companies the following year. An agreement was subsequently reached to remove the broad gauge rail, and from then on all GW services were formed of standard gauge locomotives and stock.

At around the same time, the London & South Western Railway was in the process of building its Kensington to Richmond line *(See Hammersmith Grove Road pp.84-85.)*, and in doing so impinged upon the site of the H&CR terminus. Therefore a new station, with standard gauge track only, was opened a few hundred feet to the south on 1st December 1868 and the original was closed.

Metropolitan Railway 4-4-0T No 4 (formerly named *Mercury*) stands at Hammersmith around 1865, with the mixed gauge track in evidence.

Shepherd's Bush

Shepherd's Bush was one of the original intermediate stations on the Hammersmith & City Railway, and opened with the line on 13th June 1864.

Its entrance was sited on the west side of Railway Approach, and was rather awkwardly positioned between two main thoroughfares. From the booking hall, which was positioned within a viaduct arch, stairs ascended to the two wooden platforms above.

The line was electrified in 1906, and various improvements were subsequently planned. Amongst these was the replacement of Shepherd's Bush with new stations on either side. That to the north carried the same name, whilst that to the south became Goldhawk Road.

Both of these were brought into use on 1st April 1914, when the original station closed. The platforms and attendant buildings were demolished in 1915, although the stairways went the previous year, no doubt to deter trespassing. The former booking hall was retained however, and converted into an office to serve the new retail market which opened in Railway Approach on 29th June 1914.

The former street level accommodation, in use as a market office in 1995.

White City

A view of the station, looking towards central London on 14th November 1940, after the viaduct and part of the eastbound platform had been damaged by bombing.

Opened as Wood Lane (Exhibition) Station on 1st May 1908, this station had its entrance on the north-western side of Macfarlane Road. As its original name implied, it was constructed to serve the Franco British Exhibition of that year, and contemporary Metropolitan Railway publicity boasted it was "The only station right in the grounds".

It was retained after the exhibition closed on 31st October 1908, but within a couple of years traffic began to decline. It was therefore closed from 1st November 1914, but remained intact, and was reopened for one day only on 5th November 1920 as 'Wood Lane (White City) to serve a motor show. From then on it was opened on an "as required" basis mainly in connection with greyhound racing, which was held at White City Stadium.

It was renamed White City on 23rd November 1947, but was last used on 24th October 1959. The following day, one of its platforms was damaged by fire, and the station was permanently closed. It was announced in the Spring of 1961 that it was to be demolished, and it disappeared soon after.

LONDON TRANSPORT

Issued subject to the Bye-Laws,
Regulations and Conditions of L.T.
Exec. Available day of issue only.

WHITE CITY (M)

TO any one of L.T. stations shown on fares list at
a SINGLE
FARE of

WhiteCity(M **1/5** WhiteCity·M

1/5   1/5

0376   0376

The station in its later days.
Above : **The eastbound side.**
Below : **The westbound side.**

Charing Cross

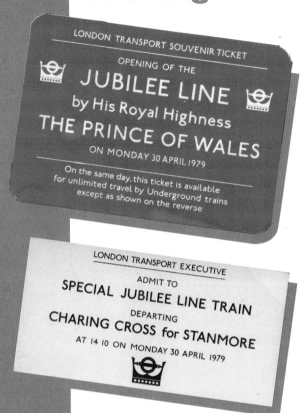

LONDON TRANSPORT SOUVENIR TICKET

OPENING OF THE

JUBILEE LINE

by His Royal Highness

THE PRINCE OF WALES

ON MONDAY 30 APRIL 1979

On the same day, this ticket is available
for unlimited travel by Underground trains
except as shown on the reverse

LONDON TRANSPORT EXECUTIVE

ADMIT TO

SPECIAL JUBILEE LINE TRAIN

DEPARTING

CHARING CROSS for STANMORE

AT 14 10 ON MONDAY 30 APRIL 1979

Following an official opening by HRH The Prince of Wales on the previous day, public services on the Jubilee Line between Charing Cross and Stanmore commenced on 1st May 1979.

The route had been planned as The Fleet Line, but its name was changed during construction, in honour of The Queen's Silver Jubilee.

Although the section linking Charing Cross with Baker Street was new, the remainder of the route had recently been part of the Bakerloo Line.

When the Jubilee Line was extended to Stratford however, the new route branched off near Green Park, and the section into Charing Cross closed after traffic on Friday 19th November 1999.

The Jubilee Line terminus at Charing Cross on its last day, with a train departing for Stanmore.

The Jubilee line will no longer serve Charing Cross after Friday 19 November

Through services start on Saturday 20 November

continued over....

The station on Friday 19th November, with closure notices visible on the wall to the left.

The Jubilee Line circulating area at Charing Cross, with the passageway to Platform 4 on the left, and Platform 3 to the right.

Lords

This station was opened as St. John's Wood Road on 13th April 1868, and was one of two intermediate passing places on the otherwise single track Metropolitan & Saint John's Wood Railway. This nominally independent company was absorbed by the larger Metropolitan Railway in 1882, and during the same year, its line was doubled throughout.

The station was extremely busy during the cricket season, due to its proximity to Lord's ground, and in the 1920s was deemed worthy of a substantial rebuild.

A new street level building, designed by architect C.W. Clark replaced the original, whilst a concrete and iron mezzanine floor was erected above the platforms to provide space for some lock-up garages.

The station was renamed St. John's Wood from 1st April 1925, and six months later, Clark's new building was completed.

Outside the cricket season traffic levels were poor, and the station's opening hours were reduced from 1st October 1929. Its platforms were subsequently lengthened to take eight car trains, but when a plan to extend the Bakerloo Line from Baker Street to Finchley Road was authorised, its days became numbered.

Following a suggestion from the Marylebone Cricket Club, it was renamed Lords on 11th June 1939, but its life under this guise proved very short, as it closed when the Bakerloo Line Extension opened on 20th November the same year, with a new station nearby named St. John's Wood.

It was thought that Lords may have been retained and used during the cricket season, but it was damaged during the Second World War, and its closure proved permanent.

A track level view of St. John's Wood Road, prior to the 1920s alterations. The walls were covered in a myriad of advertisements, which must have made reading the station's name on the platform bench very difficult for unfamiliar passengers.

C.W. Clark's 1925 street level building stood on the south side of St. John's Wood Road, close to the junction with Park Road, and survived until the late 1960s before it was demolished.

During rebuilding, the original iron and glass overall roof was retained and used as shelter for the garage accommodation below. This is the scene on 16th November 1940 after the premises were damaged in an air raid.

A view looking along the footbridge on 16th November 1940, showing some of the damage sustained from bombing. The directional signs were still in position on the wall to the left, possibly because it was originally intended to retain the station for cricket traffic. Considering the premises had already been closed for a year, the survival of posters is a little surprising, although with the country at war, there were obviously more important tasks than taking these down!

1 0000
3rd Cl   LT   ()
LORDS
5d to Uxbridge Road
    (change Baker St and
    via Ladbroke Grove)
Aldgate
Aldgate East
Neasden
Goldhawk Road
Arsenal
Barons Court
Old Street. Oval
Liverpool St (CL)
Wood Lane (CL)
Sloane Square
Walham Green
5d   or intermediately
LORDS
00000

Issued subject to the Bye-
Laws, Regulations and
Conditions of the Board.
Available day of issue only.

Marlborough Road

Marlborough Road station was opened on the Metropolitan & Saint John's Wood Railway on 13th April 1868, and had its street level building at the corner of Finchley Road and Queen's Grove.

The station changed little over the years, even after the line was electrified at the beginning of 1905, although its platforms were lengthened in the early 1930s.

It was seemingly little used by this time, as its opening hours had been substantially reduced from 1st October 1929.

The new tube station at St. John's Wood on the Bakerloo Line Extension between Baker Street and Finchley Road was opened on 20th November 1939. Marlborough Road, being rendered superfluous, was closed from the same date.

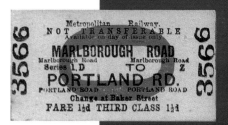

The street level building as seen from Finchley Road in evening sunshine during 1966. Remains of the station's erstwhile overall roof can be seen in the shadows on the left.

The platforms at St. John's Wood Road (later Lords), Marlborough Road and Swiss Cottage were all originally covered by glass and iron overall roofs, but the remains of that at Marlborough Road outlived the others. Here they are seen in 1966, not long before the skeletal girders were removed.

The street level building still survives, and has altered little since this photograph was taken in 1965. It was converted into a restaurant in the early 1970s, and although there have been changes of management, it continues to serve this purpose today.

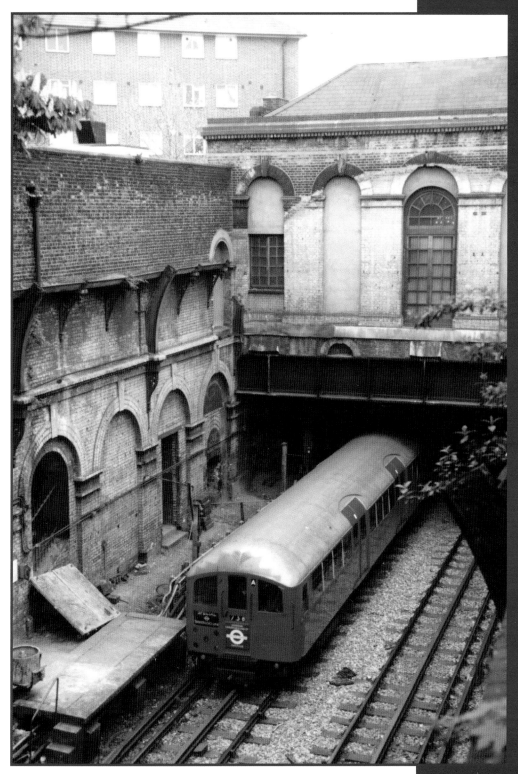

A special train formed of 1938 tube stock passes the remains of Marlborough Road station on Sunday 12th May 1985. The outline of the former overall roof can clearly be seen on the rear of the street level building.

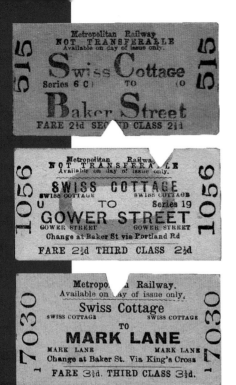

Swiss Cottage

When opened on 13th April 1868, Swiss Cottage was the terminus of the Metropolitan & Saint John's Wood Railway. This ceased to be the case after 30th June 1879, when the line was extended to West Hampstead, although the station remained largely unaltered.

In the 1920s however, the Metropolitan Railway decided to demolish the original street level building on the west side of Finchley Road, and replace it with a shopping arcade incorporating three station entrances. A little later, the platforms, which by then were completely in tunnel, were extended to take eight car trains.

When the Bakerloo Extension between Baker Street and Finchley Road was opened, the LPTB intended to retain the former Metropolitan station at Swiss Cottage as an interchange, but the connection proved to be short lived, as closure came from 18th August 1940.

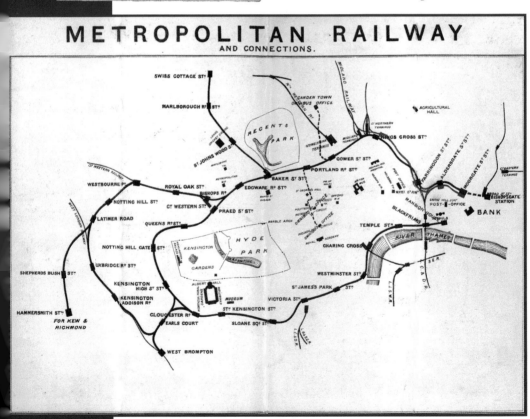

A map of the 1870s, showing the Metropolitan & Saint John's Wood Railway terminating at Swiss Cottage.

The rebuilding of Swiss Cottage station, carried out under the direction of C. W. Clark, was completed by 30th September 1929. The arcade occupied the corner of Finchley Road and Belsize Road, and was finished in white faience tiling. This view shows the station entrance facing onto Belsize Road in the early 1930s, with a sign directing passengers to the new ticket hall which was located below street level.

Clark's building survived into the late 1960s, although since 1940 had only served the Bakerloo Line. This view shows its frontage onto Finchley Road immediately prior to demolition. Very little now survives of the old Metropolitan station, although platform remains can be glimpsed from a passing train.

Preston Road for Uxendon

On 21st May 1908, the Metropolitan Railway opened a halt on the east side of Preston Road largely to serve the Uxendon Shooting School Club.

It consisted of two 260ft platforms, with small shelters on either side, and a booking office at street level.

At first the surrounding district was still fairly rural, and trains only called when requested. This sometimes resulted in drivers failing to notice waiting passengers, and passing by without stopping. Therefore it was arranged that when passengers wished to join a train, they would be accompanied by the booking clerk, who had to leave his office, then descend to the appropriate platform with a red flag.

As the area developed, it became apparent that the facilities offered by the halt were less than ideal, so improved premises were planned. In 1929, the Metropolitan Railway acquired Parliamentary Authority to widen its formation between Wembley Park and Harrow-on-the-Hill from two tracks to four. Whilst work was underway, a new station, with an island platform was erected at Preston Road to serve the local lines on the opposite side of the bridge. The new up platform was brought into use on 22nd November 1931, followed by the down on 3rd January 1932, and from this date, the original halt was officially closed.

The simple wooden halt at Preston Road for Uxendon, looking towards Harrow-on-the-Hill in its final days. After closure on 3rd January 1932, it was completely demolished, and no traces now remain.

Beyond Aylesbury

On 23rd September 1868, a small independent company opened a line to link the Great Western Railway at Aylesbury with Verney Junction on the route between Bletchley and Buckingham. It was known as the Aylesbury & Buckingham Railway, and may have remained a purely local affair, had it not have been for the intervention of the Metropolitan Railway chairman, Sir Edward William Watkin. Watkin, whose railway involvement was not restricted to the Metropolitan, had aspirations to transform London's pioneer underground route into a main line. The Met was eventually extended to its own station in Brook Street, Aylesbury on 1st September 1892, but was later connected to the GWR station, therefore allowing Brook Street to be closed. Local Metropolitan services began operating to Verney Junction on 1st April 1894, with through trains between Verney Junction and Baker Street following on 1st January 1897.

From 1st December 1899, the Metropolitan took over the operation of a branch linking Quainton Road with Brill. This originated as the Wotton Tramway, and had served a sparsely populated area since passenger services were introduced in 1872.

Watkin's dream to turn the Metropolitan into a main line railway never succeeded, although in June 1910, a pair of Pullman cars, named *Mayflower* and *Galatea* were introduced on certain 'long distance' services, including some on the Verney Junction line. These vehicles remained in service until October 1939, but by then both the Verney and Brill branches had succumbed to closure. The Quainton Road-Brill service was abandoned from 1st December 1935, and regular Metropolitan passenger trains ceased to link Aylesbury with Verney Junction after 6th July 1936.

The former junction station at Quainton Road was used by British Railways until March 1963, and now accommodates the Buckinghamshire Railway Centre, with its collection of locomotives and rolling stock.

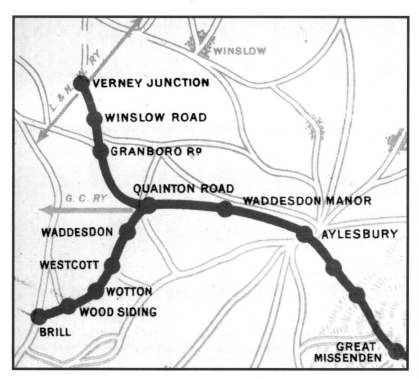

Part of a Metropolitan Railway map from 1924, showing the lines beyond Aylesbury. From 10th September 1961, all London Transport trains terminated at Amersham, and the section west of there was transferred to British Railways with services to and from Marylebone. The former Great Central Railway main line, which is shown as a westward pointing arrow from Quainton Road closed in September 1966.

The Brill branch was latterly served by old Metropolitan Railway locomotives made redundant from central London by electrification in the early years of the twentieth century. Here, a train from Quainton Road has just arrived at the terminus in the 1930s.

Metropolitan & Great Central
(324)   Joint Committee.

Wotton, O. & A. T.
TO
MARYLEBONE
(G.C.R.)

The line between Aylesbury and Verney Junction was originally single, but a second track was brought into use from 1st January 1897. This is Winslow Road station looking towards London, possibly in its final decade. The formation was again singled in 1939, three years after closure to passengers, but continued to be used by freight traffic until complete abandonment on 8th September 1947.

Verney Junction took its name from a local landowner, and was located in a very rural area. It is seen here in LPTB days with 4-4-4T No 103 about to depart with a train for Baker Street. After Metropolitan services ceased, Verney Junction remained open for the use of Oxford-Cambridge line trains, but when these were withdrawn from 1st January 1968, the station closed.

King's Cross St. Pancras

Although two of its four platform faces remain open, this station has been included as it is no longer served by Underground trains.

It opened with the first section of the Metropolitan Railway on 10th January 1863, and had its entrance on the east side of Grays Inn Road. It remained little altered until 1911/12, when LCC tramway electrification work resulted in a replacement street level building being provided at the corner of Pentonville Road and Kings Cross Bridge. At the same time, the fine but ageing overall roof was removed, and umbrella awnings were erected instead.

When opened, the station was named simply King's Cross, but in 1925 it became King's Cross & St. Pancras. A further renaming took place in 1933, when the "&" was dropped, shortening the title to King's Cross St. Pancras.

The LPTB decided to close the Circle Line platforms, and replace them with a new station to the west, which would allow better interchange with the Northern and Piccadilly lines. The platforms used by LMSR and LNER trains on the north side of the premises would not be affected however, and therefore remain open.

The station was damaged by enemy action in October 1940, but the Circle Line platforms did not officially close until 14th March the following year, when their replacements were opened.

The remaining part of the station was completely closed in 1979, but reopened as King's Cross Midland City on 11th July 1983. It was renamed King's Cross Thameslink on 16th May 1988, and remains as such at the time of writing.

The original street level entrance, as it appeared in 1910, shortly before its demolition. Behind it can be seen part of the iron and glass overall roof, which boasted a span of 80ft.

The new street level building had stairs from both Pentonville Road and King's Cross bridge, which led to a sub-surface booking hall. After closure, the building was converted for use as shops, and still survives. At the time of its construction, an entrance was positioned further east along Pentonville Road to serve the Widened Line platforms. Although completely rebuilt and enlarged, this still provides access to King's Cross Thameslink.

As part of the central island has been incorporated into King's Cross Thameslink, the only platform to be completely abandoned is that which served the westbound Circle Line. This view looks west, and shows it in 1977. For many years paper stickers still clung to the retaining wall stating 'Station Closed'.

Hillingdon

Hillingdon station was opened by the Metropolitan Railway on 10th December 1923, as a halt to serve new housing developments in the locality.

The entrance on the west side of Long Lane comprised a small half-timbered ticket hut, and open-fronted waiting shelters were provided on both platforms.

As passenger levels increased so did complaints about the frugal facilities which the premises offered. Eventually, the Met agreed to undertake improvements, and these were completed by 30th April 1931. The waiting shelters now had enclosed fronts, and the platforms were provided with canopies.

From April 1934 the suffix 'Swakeleys' was added to the station name, but this was not used consistently.

The station was resited to the south-west on 29th June 1992 in connection with expansion of the adjoining A40 Western Avenue, and the earlier premises were later demolished.

The up platform in 1931, looking towards London, showing one of the waiting shelters prior to rebuilding.

From closure until 21st December 1992, the platforms of the old station were retained as means of access to the new. Here they are seen from the present premises soon after the changeover.

The original terminus at Uxbridge was opened on 4th July 1904, and until 1st January the following year, when public electric services began, it was served by Metropolitan Railway steam trains.

It was situated off the south-eastern side of Belmont Road, and comprised two platforms. It was laid out in the manner of a through station, in anticipation of the line being extended to High Wycombe, but this never took place, and it remained a terminus to the end of its days.

From 1st March 1910, the Metropolitan services were joined by those of the Metropolitan District Railway, but from 23rd October 1933, the latter were replaced by the Piccadilly Line.

The station was not very well located for the town centre, and was replaced by completely new premises in the High Street on 4th December 1938.

The original terminus was used for a number of years as a warehouse, but its site was subsequently redeveloped.

Uxbridge

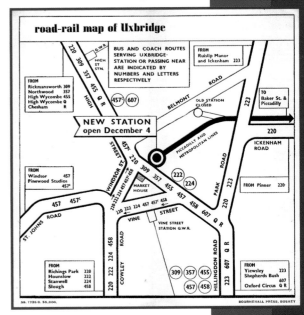

LPTB leaflet of 1938 showing the location of the new station in relationship to its predecessor.

The derelict station as it appeared in the 1950s, when it was being used for storage by a local greengrocer.

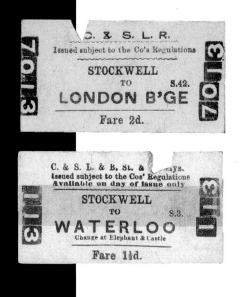

Stockwell

Built as the southern terminus of the pioneering City & South London Railway, Stockwell station was brought into public use on 18th December 1890.

Originally the company, then known as the City of London & Southwark Subway, intended its line for cable haulage, and Stockwell was planned as having a single track, with a platform either side. With the subsequent change to electric traction this was changed however, and it opened with two tracks served by a central island.

In July 1890, the company received Parliamentary authority to extend its route to Clapham Common, and Stockwell ceased to be a terminus on 3rd June 1900.

Originally the line was worked with locomotives, but these were later replaced by conventional Underground stock. As part of the modernisation programme, Stockwell closed on 29th November 1923, and did not reopen until 1st December the following year. During this time, new platforms were constructed in twin tunnels, south of the original, and the former island was abandoned. Its site is still visible from a passing train.

The CSLR was officially opened by HRH The Prince of Wales (later King Edward VII) on 4th November 1890, but public traffic did not commence until the following month. Here the royal party is seen after arrival at Stockwell.

King William Street

The City terminus of the world's first electric tube railway was ceremonially opened by HRH The Prince of Wales (later King Edward Vll) on 4th November 1890, but because of various technical problems, public traffic did not start until a few weeks later on 18th December.

Initially the City & South London Railway had been planned as the City of London & Southwark Subway, and was intended for cable haulage. This was changed prior to opening, but King William Street station was laid out in a manner perhaps more suitable for cable traction than electric.

In addition, its approaches from beneath the Thames involved sharp curves and crippling gradients, so within just two years of opening, the company decided to extend the line northwards to Moorgate Street, and cut out King William Street altogether.

The station underwent modifications in 1895 to ease operational difficulties, but it closed from 25th February 1900 when the new extension, which left the original alignment just north of Borough, was brought into use.

The station's entrance was incorporated within an existing office building at No 46 King William Street. When the Underground Group decided to dispose of this in 1930, a number of journalists were invited along to provide publicity. Down below, much still survived, including the exit passageways, which are seen here.

Originally King William Street was served by a single track, with a platform on either side. In 1895 this was changed to two roads and a central island, and it remained like this until closure. The station is seen here in 1930, when even the derelict wooden signal box remained standing.

When visited by the press in 1930, there were still some old posters clinging to the walls. No 46 King William Street was subsequently sold for redevelopment, and demolished in 1933 to provide a site for an office block known as Regis House. This survived until 1995, but has since been replaced by a building of the same name.

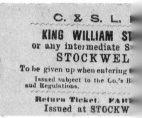

In 1940, the owners of Regis House took out a tenancy on the former station tunnel, and converted it into an air raid shelter. This was provided with two floors, and although many relics must have disappeared in the process, the tiled tunnel walls were retained.

City Road

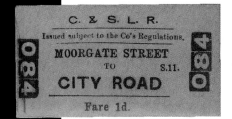

City Road station opened with the City & South London Railway extension from Moorgate Street to Angel on 17th November 1901.

It was located between Old Street and Angel, and consisted of two platforms. Its surface building stood at the corner of City Road and Moreland Street, and passengers gained access to the trains by means of two lifts.

It was never well used, and as early as 1908, the company were considering its closure. It remained open however, but its days were numbered.

The CSLR became part of the Underground Group on 1st January 1913, and so that standardised rolling stock could be used, the bore of the running tunnels had to be enlarged. The section of line north of Moorgate Street closed for rebuilding on 9th August 1922, and although this subsequently reopened, City Road remained closed. The platforms were later removed, and the former platform tunnels were converted for use as an air raid shelter in 1941.

An early Underground Group map, with the CSLR indicated in black.

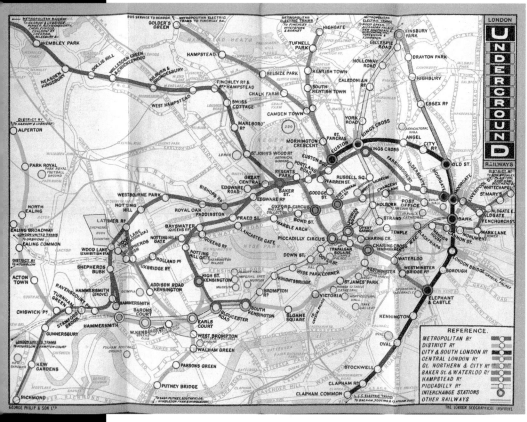

The tower of a ventilation shaft was subsequentl[y] added to the street level building, but otherwise it remained little altered for many years after closure. Partial demolition took place around the 1970s, but a fragment of it stil[l] survives

Although the platforms have long-since disappeared, the former station tunnels retain their white tiling, and can be seen from a passing train. This view shows the remains as they appeared in the 1980s.

South Kentish Town

Prior to opening on 22nd June 1907, this station on the Charing Cross Euston & Hampstead Railway was known as Castle Road. In fact, this was the name which was fired onto the platform tiling, but the company changed its mind, and painted it out before services commenced.

It was never well used, and when it closed during a strike at Lots Road power station on 5th June 1924, it never reopened.

In 1940, the former platform tunnels were adapted for use as air raid shelters, and equipped with bunks and a first aid post. These fittings were removed when hostilities ended however, and the station returned to its slumber.

The platforms were removed at an unknown date, but according to an article in *The Railway World* for December 1954, the wall tiling could *"still be seen from passing trains."*

The street level building, designed by Leslie W. Green still stands, and is currently used as commercial premises. It is located at the corner of Kentish Town Road and Castle Place, and externally has changed little since closure.

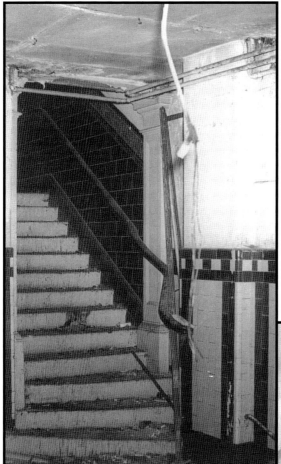

The stairway from the street level building, partially clad in dark green tiling led to the upper lift landing which was tiled in cream and dark red.

The lifts were removed many years ago, and the shaft was plugged, but the lower lift landing retained many of its original features.

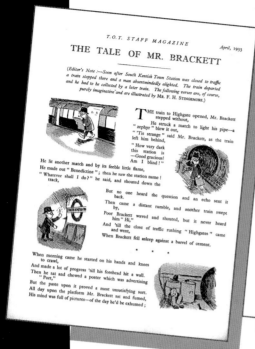
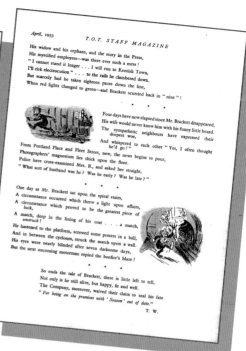

T.O.T. STAFF MAGAZINE   April, 1933

THE TALE OF MR. BRACKETT

(Editor's Note :—Soon after South Kentish Town Station was closed to traffic
a train stopped there and a man absentmindedly alighted. The train departed
and he had to be collected by a later train. The following verses are, of course,
purely imaginative and are illustrated by Mr. F. H. STINGEMORE.)

THE train to Highgate opened, Mr. Brackett
stepped without,
He struck a match to light his pipe—a
" zephyr " blew it out,
" 'Tis strange " said Mr. Brackett, as the train
left him behind,
" How very dark
this station is
—Good gracious!
Am I blind ! "

He lit another match and by its feeble little flame,
He made out " Benedictine " ; then he saw the station name !
" Whatever shall I do? " he said, and shouted down the
track,

But no one heard the question and an echo sent it
back.
Then came a distant rumble, and another train swept
by,
Poor Brackett waved and shouted, but it never heard
him " Hi,"
And 'till the close of traffic rushing " Highgates " came
and went,
When Brackett fell asleep against a barrel of cement.

*   *   *

When morning came he started on his hands and knees
to crawl,
And made a lot of progress 'till his forehead hit a wall.
Then he sat and chewed a poster which was advertising
" Port,"
But the paste upon it proved a most unsatisfying sort.
All day upon the platform Mr. Brackett sat and fumed,
His mind was full of pictures—of the day he'd be exhumed ;

April, 1933   T.O.T. STAFF MAGAZINE

His widow and his orphans, and the story in the Press,
His mystified employers—was there ever such a mess !
" I cannot stand it longer . . . . I will run to Kentish Town,
I'll risk electrocution " . . . . to the rails he clambered down.
But scarcely had he taken eighteen paces down the line,
When red lights changed to green—and Brackett scurried back in " nine " !

*   *   *

Four days have now elapsed since Mr. Brackett disappeared,
His wife would never know him with his funny little beard.
The sympathetic neighbours have expressed their
deepest woe,
And whispered to each other " Yes, I often thought
he'd go ! "
From Portland Place and Fleet Street, now, the news begins to pour,
Photographers' magnesium lies thick upon the floor.
Police have cross-examined Mrs. B., and asked her straight,
" What sort of husband was he ? Was he early ? Was he late ? "

*   *   *

One day as Mr. Brackett sat upon the spiral stairs,
A circumstance occurred which threw a light upon affairs,
A circumstance which proved to be the greatest piece of
luck,
A match, deep in the lining of his coat . . . a match,
unstruck !
He hastened to the platform, screwed some posters in a ball,
And in between the cyclones, struck the match upon a wall.
His eyes were nearly blinded after seven darksome days,
But the next oncoming motorman espied the bonfire's blaze !

*   *   *

So ends the tale of Brackett, there is little left to tell,
Not only is he still alive, but happy, fit and well.
The Company, moreover, waived their claim to seal his fate
" For being on the premises with ' Season ' out of date."

T. W.

An incident concerning an absent minded passenger alighting at South
Kentish Town soon after closure led to this verse being published in the
TOT staff magazine, and later inspired a story which was broadcast on the
BBC Home Service by John (later Sir John) Betjeman in 1951.

At track level the station tunnels can be seen from a passing train between
Camden Town and Kentish Town, but their cream and dark red tiling has
been largely obliterated by paint.

North End

Passengers travelling between Hampstead and Golders Green on today's Northern Line may look out into the tunnel, and see what appears to be the remains of a disused station. In fact, what they are seeing is the site of a station which was partially constructed by the Charing Cross Euston & Hampstead Railway, but abandoned before completion. It was to be named North End, and would have had a street level building on the north side of Hampstead Way, opposite Wyldes Farmhouse.

The fact that much of its immediate surroundings consisted of conserved open land meant that there was little chance of development in the area, so the project was cancelled. By this time, some work had been carried out at track level, but nothing was erected above.

The unfinished station later became known by staff as 'Bull & Bush' after the nearby public house featured in Florrie Forde's famous music hall song.

A floodgate control room was installed there in the 1950s, when access from the street was finally provided, although the site originally intended for its building was sold for residential use in 1927.

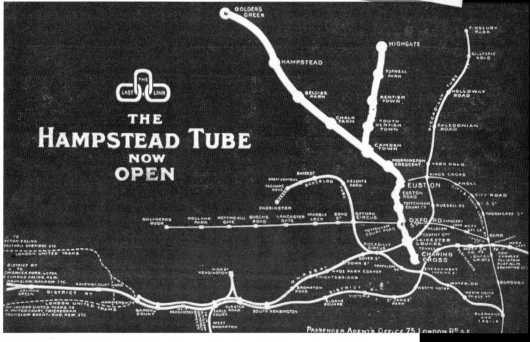

A 1907 map of the Charing Cross Euston & Hampstead Railway, or 'Hampstead Tube' as it was advertised, showing the line when opened. The aborted station at North End is of course not included.

York Road

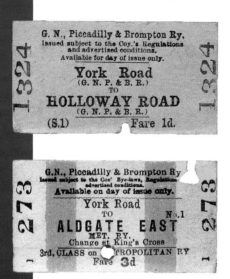

Opened on 15th December 1906, York Road was one of the original stations on the Great Northern Piccadilly & Brompton Railway.

It was located between King's Cross and Caledonian Road, and had its entrance at the corner of York Road (now York Way) and Bingfield Street.

Even in its early days it appears to have been little used, and some trains began to pass without stopping from October 1909. Sunday services were withdrawn after 5th May 1918, but apart from an extended period of disuse brought about by the General Strike in 1926, the station remained open for weekday traffic until 19th September 1932, when it was permanently closed.

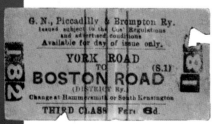

The fine street level building, designed by Leslie W. Green still survives, and is a fine example of the architect's work. Its frontage was renovated in 1989, and since then the remains of the original lettering, including the station name have been clearly visible.

The platform tiling at York Road was carried out by G. Woolliscroft & Sons of Hanley in Staffordshire, and was made up of white with maroon and brick red patterning. The majority of this, including the tiled name panels, has been painted over in matt grey paint, but a small section remains untouched, at the Finsbury Park end of the former eastbound platform and can be glimpsed by observant passengers from passing trains.

Near this section of tiling stands a small signal cabin, which once operated a crossover immediately to the north-east of the station. The box remained operative until 25th April 1964, although by this time the crossover was very little used, having been replaced by a new one at King's Cross eight years earlier.

Aldwych

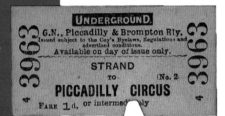

The station was opened as Strand by the Great Northern Piccadilly & Brompton Railway on 30th November 1907, but was renamed Aldwych on 9th May 1915.

It was the terminus of a 573 yard branch line from Holborn, and although well patronised by theatre goers in its early days, its fortunes soon fell into decline.

One of its two platforms was little used after 1912, and was later closed completely.

Services over the branch were suspended during the Second World War from 22nd September 1940 until 1st July 1946. During these years the tunnels were used as an air raid shelter, and also to store art treasures from the British Museum.

The need for lift replacement hastened the station's demise, and final closure came on 3rd October 1994.

The station occupied an L shaped site which previously accomodated the Royal Strand Theatre. This is the Surrey Street facade just prior to completion in 1907.

The station entrance which faced onto the Strand was a modest affair. When first built both this, and the Surrey Street facade carried the legend 'Piccadilly Tube', but the latter word seemingly met with disapproval so it was changed to 'Rly' at an early date.

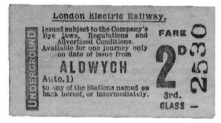

For much of its existence Aldwych station was served by a shuttle service which operated to and from Holborn. Here, one of these workings is seen in the 1950s, when the trains were formed of 'Standard Stock'. Although Aldwych had no direct interchange facilities, a hanging sign directed alighting passengers towards the nearby District Line station at Temple.

The abandoned platform, little served after 1912, and closed completely from 16th August 1917, was used by LT design staff to provide mock-up facilities for new station decors. This view dates from the 1960s, and shows the style of tiling later adopted for the Victoria Line to the left. By way of contrast, one of the old 'Strand' name panels is visible beneath the light near the centre.

Aldwych Station closure proposal

London Underground has today given notice that it intends to close Aldwych Station and withdraw train services on the Holborn-Aldwych branch of the Piccadilly line. The closure would be effective after the last train on 2 April 1993 if there are no objections to the proposal.

Background

London Underground's reason for wishing to close Aldwych is that the lifts (which date from 1906) are life-expired, cannot be adapted to modern safety standards, and so need to be replaced. The cost of doing so would be in the region of £3 million. Only 450 people a day use Aldwych - so the cost per person of replacing the lifts would be roughly £6,000. In addition to the operating loss the branch already causes.

At a time when the Government has just reduced the amount it promised to London Underground for capital investment on the existing network, replacing these lifts cannot be justified. Aldwych is too deep for reliance on stairs alone as a means of reaching the platform and so London Underground has taken the decision to apply to close it.

Alternative transport

There are many alternative means of reaching the area served by Aldwych Station by London Transport services on which Travelcards are valid. Holborn, Covent Garden and Temple stations are all close at hand and no fewer than nine bus routes run between Holborn Station and the Aldwych. London Underground believes these provide an ample substitute for the Tube shuttle.

What happens next?

Notices giving details of how to object formally to the proposal will be posted at Underground stations and published in the Press shortly. If no objections are received the last services will run on Friday 2 April 1993. If there are objections, these will be considered by the London Regional Passengers' Committee and the Secretary of State for Transport before a final decision is reached.

London Underground
6 January 1993

In readiness for closure, the posters were stripped from the walls, revealing the old tiled name panel underneath. This view, taken on the last night, Friday 30th September 1994, also shows the section of tunnel at the Holborn end which never received tiling, and remained unfinished throughout the station's life.

Down Street

Because of problems at its planning stage, work on constructing Down Street station was late in starting, and therefore its opening was delayed. It was brought into use on 15th March 1907, three months after public services on the Great Northern Piccadily & Brompton Railway had commenced, but from the outset traffic was very light.

It was close to both Dover Street (now Green Park), and Hyde Park Corner, which were the stations on either side, and it served a district where, even in its early days, people had access to private transport.

Certain trains began to pass without stopping after 1909, and Sunday services were withdrawn from 5th May 1918. Complete closure came fourteen years later, on 22nd May 1932.

Leslie W. Green's street level building at Down Street: right, as it is today, and below, shortly after opening.

Below street level, much of the old Down Street station survives, and of recent years, occasional public visits have been organised by the London Transport Museum. This view shows the passageway which led from the lower lift landing.

Immediately prior to the Second World War, the premises were adapted as bomb-proof office accommodation, and became the headquarters of the Railway Executive Committee. Down Street was also used by the War Cabinet on occasion, and Winston Churchill was reputedly sometimes seen walking across Green Park, en-route from Whitehall. When hostilities ended, the office partitions which had been erected within the passageways were removed, but traces of them still remain, as seen here.

G. N., Piccadilly & Brompton Ry.
Issued subject to the Co.'s Regulations
and advertised conditions.
Available for day of issue only.

Down Street

TO

RUSSELL SQUARE

S. 1)   Fare 2d.

5787   5787

The western ends of the platforms at Down Street were demolished to facilitate the construction of a new reversing siding soon after closure, and much of the original maroon and cream tiling was later obliterated with matt grey paint. Traces of original signs still exist however, and examples are shown here.

There are also various signs and other reminders of the station's wartime role.

Brompton Road

Brompton Road was situated between Knightsbridge and South Kensington, on the Great Northern, Piccadilly & Brompton Railway, and opened with the line on 15th December 1906.

Although convenient for the Brompton Oratory and the Victoria & Albert Museum, it was never well patronised, and from October 1909 some trains passed without stopping. Before leaving either Knightsbridge or South Kensington, staff on these services would yell *"Passing Brompton Road!"*, and this call became so familiar that it gave its name to a West End farce in 1928.

The station closed from 4th May 1926 due to the General Strike, and did not reopen until 4th October the same year. When first brought back into use, trains only called on weekdays, but Sunday services were restored on 2nd January 1927.

By then however, its days were numbered, and when the newly rebuilt Knightsbridge station was provided with an additional entrance fairly nearby, Brompton Road closed from 30th July 1934.

694 | 694

G. N., Piccadilly & Brompton Ry.
Issued subject to the Coy.'s Regulations
and advertised conditions.
Available for day of issue only.

Brompton Road
TO
BARON'S COURT
(8.1A)   Fare 2d.

The station occupied an L shaped site with its entrance and exit facing Brompton Road. This is the frontage soon after opening.

Just prior to the outbreak of the Second World War, the street level building, together with liftshafts and certain passageways was sold to the War Office for use by the 1st Anti-Aircraft Division. This view shows the operations room which was located in one of the lift shafts.

Although the platforms themselves have been removed, and their site hidden from passing trains by brick walls, much of the old tiling remains, including some of the original name panels. This view was taken in December 1996.

G. N., Piccadilly & Brompton Ry.
Issued subject to the Co.'s Regulations
and advertised conditions.
Available for day of issue only.

Brompton Road
TO
GREAT CENTRAL
(B. St. & W. R.)
Change at Piccadilly Circus.

FARE **3d.**

1070

1070

The station frontage was demolished in 1972 to facilitate a road widening scheme, but a section of the building facing Cottage Place still survives, and is seen here in December 1999.

Although not visible from a passing train, the tiled walls of the former platform tunnels remain intact in places. The colour scheme employed at Brompton Road was cream and white, with patterning picked out in brown and green.

Northfields & Little Ealing

On 16th April 1908, the Metropolitan District Railway opened Northfield (Ealing) Halt between South Ealing and Boston Road (now Boston Manor) on the Hounslow line.

As suburban development along this route had been slow to develop, the premises were very basic, and comprised a street level ticket hut, serving a pair of 300ft platforms.

With traffic increasing however, the halt proved inadequate, so it was rebuilt as a full station, and renamed Northfields & Little Ealing on 11th December 1911.

In time, it was decided to extend Piccadilly Line trains to Hounslow West, but before this could be done, a number of improvements had to be made. Amongst these was the laying of additional tracks between Acton Town and Northfields, and the provision of a new depot near Boston Manor. To facilitate these changes, it proved necessary to resite Northfields station eastwards to the opposite side of the road.

The new station was opened, albeit still unfinished, on 19th May 1932. Its predecessor closed on the same date, and was subsequently demolished.

Northfield Halt, looking east in its early days. The Hounslow line was electrified in 1905

The entrance was located on the west side of Northfields Lane (now Northfield Avenue). This is the street level building of the 1911 station.

A view which is believed to date from the 1920s, showing Northfields & Little Ealing station looking towards Acton Town.

Osterley

Osterley station was opened by the Hounslow & Metropolitan Railway on 1st May 1883, but its services were provided by the Metropolitan District Railway from the outset.

Its street level building was located on the west side of Thornbury Road, and from here, stairs descended to the platforms below.

It is known that the board on the frontage displayed the name as 'Osterley Park and Spring Grove', but it appears that this was never shown on MDR tickets, even if variations of it sometimes appeared on through bookings from other companies.

The original Osterley station closed on 25th March 1934, when it was replaced by new premises facing onto the Great West Road.

The original Osterley station looking east on 31st December 1930.

The street level building still stands, and has changed little since this photograph was taken in the 1930s.

The canopies and stairways were demolished in 1957, but the platforms remain in position. This view, which includes an enthusiasts' special train formed of 1938 tube stock, was taken on 12th May 1985.

Hounslow Town

The Hounslow & Metropolitan Railway opened this terminus on 1st May 1883. It was originally called Hounslow, but was renamed Hounslow Town the following year. The company wanted to extend the line to form a link with the London & South Western Railway, but the LSWR objected to this, and the scheme failed to materialise.

The HMR, which was worked by the Metropolitan District Railway from the outset, later extended its system to Hounslow Barracks (later Hounslow West), leaving its original terminus as a rather superfluous appendage. It therefore closed from 1st April 1886, but was reopened on 1st March 1903.

In anticipation of electrification, an additional spur was added, to provide access from the Hounslow Barracks end, and this was opened to coincide with the new electric service on 13th June 1905. The method of running all trains by way of the old terminus proved far from satisfactory however, and it was permanently closed from 2nd May 1909.

Hounslow Town station was later demolished, and redeveloped as a 'bus garage, but the site of the original junction can still be seen on the south side of today's Piccadilly Line between Osterley and Hounslow East.

This section of a Metropolitan District Railway map of August 1907 shows the route taken by MDR trains in the years immediately following electrification.

On closure the station was replaced by a new Hounslow Town on the direct line. Since 1st December 1925, this second station has been named Hounslow East.

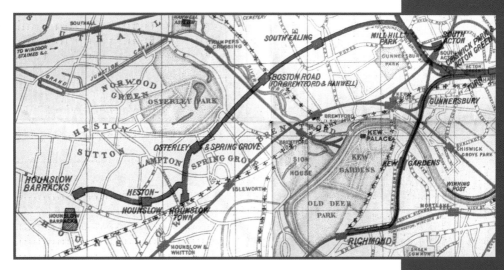

The direct route between Osterley and Heston Hounslow, was out of regular public use from 13th June 1905 until 2nd May 1909, and was therefore not included on this map.

Hounslow West

UNDERGROUND
DISTRICT RAILWAY.
Issued subject to the Companies' Bye Laws,
Regulations and advertised Conditions.

Hounslow Barracks (1)
TO
HOUNSLOW TOWN

3RD CLASS   FARE 1 1/2 d
Available day of issue only.

3179   3179

DISTRICT RAILWAY.
Issued subject to the Companies' Bye Laws,
Regulations and advertised Conditions.
HOUNSLOW WEST
(1)   TO
HOUNSLOW EAST
or intermediately
1 1/2 d THIRD CLASS FARE 1 1/2 d
Available day of issue only

6282   6282

This view shows Hounslow West terminus in the early 1930s, soon after the introduction of Piccadilly Line trains. The original platform can be seen to the right, but that on which the photographer was standing was a new island, added in 1929.

Originally named Hounslow Barracks, the station was opened on 21st July 1884 as terminus of the Hounslow & Metropolitan Railway.

It lay at the end of an extension which diverged from the original Hounslow Town line at Lampton Junction, and consisted of a single platform. In fact, the line which served it was single, although the formation was built to a sufficient width for it to be doubled at a later stage if required. This later took place, but the final stretch into Hounslow Barracks remained single until 1929.

The route was electrified by the Metropolitan District Railway in 1905, but it would be some years before any substantial improvements were made at the station. The first sign of change came on 1st December 1925 when it was renamed Hounslow West, then four years later it was substantially enlarged.

Piccadilly Line services were extended to serve Hounslow West on 8th February 1932, and for over three decades shared the station with the District Line. District trains were withdrawn from the route after 9th October 1964 however, and thereafter it was served by the Piccadilly Line only.

An extension of the branch to serve Heathrow Airport necessitated the provision of a through station on the new route. The old terminal platforms were last used on 11th July 1975, and were subsequently demolished to provide space for a car park, although the main building, completed in 1931 to the design of Charles Holden remains in use.

Park Royal & Twyford Abbey

The original Park Royal station was located on the south side of Twyford Abbey Road, and opened on 23rd June 1903. The premises were very basic, and comprised a pair of wooden platforms linked by a footbridge.

As its name implied, the station was intended to serve the 102 acre Royal Agricultural Showground which lay immediately to its east.

The route between Hanger Lane Junction and South Harrow on which the station was situated, was initially served by the Metropolitan District Railway, but from 4th July 1932 it became part of the Piccadilly Line. In preparation for this change, it was decided to build a new Park Royal station about 30 chains to the east, and then close the original. The new premises were a vast improvement on those in Twyford Abbey Road, and were brought into use on 6th July 1931 as a direct replacement for them.

Being a fairly flimsy structure, the original station was easily demolished, and no tangible traces of it now remain.

Although the original station was officially named Park Royal & Twyford Abbey, the full title did not appear on its final nameboards, nor seemingly on MDR tickets which were issued there.
This view shows the stairs from street level which led up to the corrugated iron ticket office.

Uxbridge Road

Uxbridge Road was opened by the West London Railway on 1st November 1869, and was located north of Kensington Addison Road (now Olympia) near the site of an earlier WLR Shepherds Bush station which had opened and closed in 1844.

In addition to West London Line trains between Clapham Junction and Willesden Junction, Uxbridge Road was also served by the Metropolitan Railway, which reached it by means of a connecting spur off the Hammersmith & City route to the south-west of Latimer Road. This spur opened on 1st July 1864, and for many years formed part of 'The Middle Circle'. By way of this, Metropolitan trains could diverge near Latimer Road, then after calling at Uxbridge Road and Addison Road, arrive at Earl's Court.

Uxbridge Road station was closed on 20th October 1940, and the spur lost its passenger services from the same date. It was retained for freight traffic until 1st March 1954, but was then lifted.

The Latimer Road - Earl's Court route, together with Uxbridge Road, last appeared on an Underground pocket map in 1947, seven years after the station closed. Today the only section still used by Underground services is that between Earl's Court and Kensington Olympia.

The erstwhile junction at Latimer Road on 27th September 1957, after the spur had been lifted. Although much of the formation has since disappeared, its one-time divergence near Latimer Road can still be seen from a passing train.

The platform buildings at Uxbridge Road were demolished by the early 1960s, and photographs of them are fairly rare. This excellent view, dating from 12th August 1956, was taken from the brake van of a Bow - Kensington Olympia freight train, and shows the northbound side.

The street level building, to the east of Shepherds Bush Green, survived until the early 1970s, when it was demolished to facilitate road alterations. At the time of writing there is talk of opening a new station on the site to serve a proposed shopping centre.

Hammersmith Grove Road

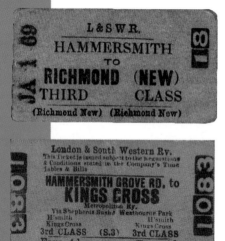

Opened as Hammersmith by the London & South Western Railway on 1st January 1869, this station was located on the line linking Kensington Addison Road (now Olympia) with Richmond.

Services were initially only provided by the LSWR, but from 1st June 1870, a connection off the Hammersmith & City Line allowed the operation of GWR trains from Bishop's Road Paddington to Richmond. These called at the LSWR Hammersmith station, but were withdrawn after just a few months on 1st November 1870. From 1st October 1877 however, the link began to be used by Metropolitan Railway Moorgate Street - Richmond trains, with GWR services making their reappearance in 1894. Passengers were subsequently wooed away by the new electric tramways, and the connection between the H&C and LSWR was finally closed from 1st January 1911.

Hammersmith station, by now in possession of the suffix 'Grove Road', or as it was sometimes known 'The Grove', continued to be used by LSWR services until closure on 5th June 1916.

Since 1877, the Metropolitan District Railway had operated over the LSWR route beyond Hammersmith to reach Richmond, and these services continued. Therefore only the section of line between Kensington and Hammersmith was actually closed, and although there was talk of bringing it back into use, it was subsequently lifted.

Passengers on today's District and Piccadilly Line trains can still see parts of the disused viaduct to the north of the formation between Hammersmith and Ravenscourt Park stations. The link with the H&C has long since disappeared however, as has the station at Hammersmith Grove Road.

A group of workmen pose on a heap of coal outside Hammersmith Grove Road station at an unknown date, seemingly whilst being entertained by the musician on the left. The main building, visible on the right stood east of Hammersmith Grove, opposite the junction with Glenthorne Road, and survived as a warehouse until 1954. At the same time, the lattice girder bridge which crossed the Grove, and can just be seen in the background, was also demolished.

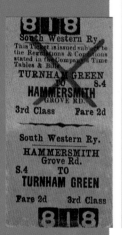

Apart from the main building, which was brick, Hammersmith Grove Road was largely constructed of wood. The upper and lower photographs are thought to date from 1920, and therefore show the premises four years after closure. To the left of the top view, a footbridge connection to the H&C Hammersmith terminus can just be seen leading from the LSWR building.

The connecting spur which allowed Metropolitan Railway trains to serve the station diverged from the H&C line a little to the north of Hammersmith terminus at the aptly named Richmond Junction. Although the connection had long since disappeared, the disused signal box lasted much longer, and it is seen here in the 1970s.

On 1st March 1883, the Metropolitan District Railway commenced working between Mansion House and Windsor, by way of a connection onto the GWR at Ealing. The service initially comprised eleven weekday trains each way, with nine on Sundays, but there was little demand, so it was cut back to four in either direction on 1st October 1884. It was withdrawn completely from 30th September 1885, and track alterations at Ealing Broadway in 1898/9 eliminated the connection completely. This view shows MDR 4-4-0T No 42 carrying a Windsor destination board. Unfortunately, the background has been painted out, but the photograph is thought to have been taken at Mill Hill Park. (now Acton Town).

This view, which was taken on 25th August 1932 shows an Ealing to Southend through train at Whitechapel.
It is formed of ex-LTSR corridor coaching stock, which was specially built for the service in 1911.

From 1st June 1910 until 1st October 1939, a service of through trains operated between Ealing Broadway and Southend. These travelled by way of the Whitechapel & Bow Railway, which had opened in 1902, and were hauled by a pair of MDR electric locomotives, generally as far as Barking where an engine from the London, Tilbury & Southend Railway would take over.

The District Deep Level Line

To relieve pressure on its most overcrowded section, the Metropolitan District Railway contemplated building a deep level tube line between Earl's Court and Mansion House. The scheme was announced in October 1896, and was envisaged to diverge from the existing tracks east of Earl's Court before descending on a 1 in 42 gradient towards Gloucester Road. It would then continue below the sub-surface MDR in a pair of 12ft 6in tubes and eventually terminate at Mansion House. It was to be electrified from the outset, and to speed up services there would be only one intermediate station. This was planned for Charing Cross (now Embankment), where the new platforms would lie 63ft below the original District Line, and these would be connected to the booking hall above by means of hydraulic lifts.

Parliamentary authority was received on 6th August 1897, but the line never materialised in its intended form. At that time, the MDR was still worked by steam, and a change of locomotives would be necessary before trains could continue onto the tube section. Because this would almost certainly cause delays if carried out at Earl's Court, it was suggested that it should take place in a stretch of covered way beneath Cromwell Road. In the event however, the plan was abandoned, although the stretch from South Kensington to Earl's Court was ultimately built as part of the Great Northern Piccadilly & Brompton Railway.

The remaining section remained largely untouched, apart from a 120ft length of station tunnel which was constructed at South Kensington in 1903. This was level with the present westbound Piccadilly Line platform, but before completion it was realised that electrification of the existing MDR would increase the line capacity through the City, and the deep level route would therefore not be required. No further work was carried out, and Parliamentary powers to build between South Kensington and Mansion House were relinquished in 1908.

The unfinished station tunnel at South Kensington, which was tiled in the style used on the various Yerkes' tube lines, served as a signalling school from 1927 to 1939. During the Second World War, part of it was equipped with electronic equipment to record any delayed action bombs which were dropped in the Thames, and threatened to breach underwater tube tunnels.

TheNorthern Heights

Probably the best known abandoned Underground project is the scheme to extend Northern Line services to Alexandra Palace and Bushey Heath. Both of these had their origins in New Works Plans of the 1930s, and had it not been for the intervention of the Second World War, they would have no doubt materialised.

The plan envisaged the London Passenger Transport Board taking over the former GNR branches to Edgware, High Barnet and Alexandra Palace, and replacing the existing steam workings with tube trains. At Edgware a connection to the existing LPTB station would be laid, and a completetly new extension built to serve Brockley Hill, Elstree (later referred to as Elstree South) and Bushey Heath.

Work continued into the early years of the War, but as the Luftwaffe raids on London intensified, the scheme was halted. Tube trains reached High Barnet on 14th April 1940, before the onset of the Blitz, and a year later, on 18th May 1941, they got to Mill Hill East. From then on however the scheme faltered, and the remaining Northern Heights projects were left unfinished.

Post-War Green Belt legislation ruled out developing the area north of Edgware, so the Bushey Heath plan was ultimately scrapped, and the line serving Alexandra Palace was latterly so little used that electrification was not deemed worthwhile. Instead it remained steam worked to the end, and closed from 5th July 1954.

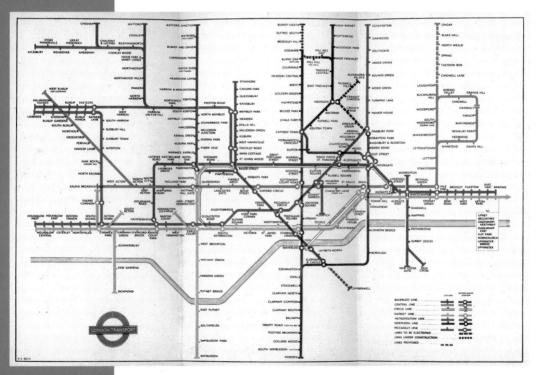

The 1949 edition of the pocket Underground map was the last to show Mill Hill East - Edgware and Bushey Heath, whilst Alexandra Palace was deleted the following year. To the south, work on extending the Bakerloo Line to Camberwell was expected to start in 1950, and be completed three years later, but this was another scheme to prove moribund.

Until 7th September 1969, it was possible to buy tickets from the British Rail booking office at Mill Hill Broadway, which were headed 'London Transport' and showed the station of origin as Mill Hill The Hale. These were valid on the 240 'bus route, and were one of the last tangible reminders of the aborted LT scheme. Mill Hill The Hale was on the LNER Edgware branch, and was within easy walking distance of the station at Mill Hill Broadway.

Although tube services reached Mill Hill East in 1941, the line between Finsbury Park and Edgware continued to be used by LNER and later BR goods trains until 1st June 1964. Here a train of LPTB 1938 Stock stands at Mill Hill East, as a steam hauled freight approaches on the non-electrified section from Edgware.

Mill Hill The Hale started life as The Hale Halt in 1906, and last saw passenger trains when the branch was closed for electrification on 11th September 1939. It was due for complete rebuilding, but only a certain amount of platform work was ever completed, as seen in this Post-War view. The bridge in the foreground carried Bunns Lane over the route, whilst that in the distance is the Midland main line.

LONDON TRANSPORT

Issued subject to the Bye-Laws, Regulations and Conditions of L.T. Board. Available day of issue only

MILL HILL (THE HALE)

To any one of L.T. stations shown on Fares list at a SINGLE FARE of

Mill Hill (The Hale) Mill Hill (The Hale)

1/3   **1/3**   1/3

Although a great deal of preparatory work was carried out on the route between Edgware and Bushey Heath, the most notable civil engineering feature was this unfinished viaduct at Brockley Hill. This would have supported the station, and a service road leading into the car park was intended to pass between the two sets of arches. The view dates from 1958, and shows the structure shortly before partial demolition. Today only the lower sections survive, and can be seen to the north of Edgware Way.

The line would have passed through Brockley Hill itself in twin tunnels, as seen here. These served as a rifle range for a while, but were bricked up in August 1953, and have since disappeared. The only other major structure erected for the line was the depot at Aldenham, between Elstree South and Bushey Heath. This was used for aircraft construction during the war, and later became well known for overhauling London's 'buses. It has since been closed and demolished.

The first station out of Finsbury Park heading towards Alexandra Palace was Stroud Green, which opened on 11th April 1881, and had its entrance on the west side of Stapleton Hall Road, just south of the junction with Ferme Park Road. This view dates from January 1966, and was taken just three months before demolition.

Further on, the line reached Crouch End, which was entered by way of a street level building on the east side of Crouch End Hill, south of the junction with Haslemere Road. The station was opened on 22nd August 1867, and remained largely unaltered, although work was latterly carried out to lower the platform height to enable use by tube services. The trackbed of the line between Finsbury Park and Highgate is now a public footpath, and although the majority of Crouch End station has disappeared, its platforms still remain.

Highgate station, which had opened with the line from Finsbury Park to Edgware on 22nd August 1867, was substantially modernised in 1940-41 when it received a new Holden designed building on its island platform, reached by a stairway from the Underground booking hall below. The tracks were used for transferring Underground stock between Drayton Park on the Northern City Line and Highgate Wood sidings until 1970. As they were not electrified, the trains had to be hauled by battery locomotives. The track was lifted in 1972, but Highgate station still survived in 1999, albeit derelict and overgrown.

Beyond Highgate, the branch to Alexandra Palace diverged from the High Barnet and Edgware routes, and soon reached Cranley Gardens. This station opened on 2nd August 1902, and is seen here in 1966, about eight years after the branch track had been removed. Its street level building stood on the west side of Muswell Hill Road, almost opposite the junction with Cranley Gardens itself, but this was demolished along with the platform remains in the late 1960s, when the site was required for redevelopment.

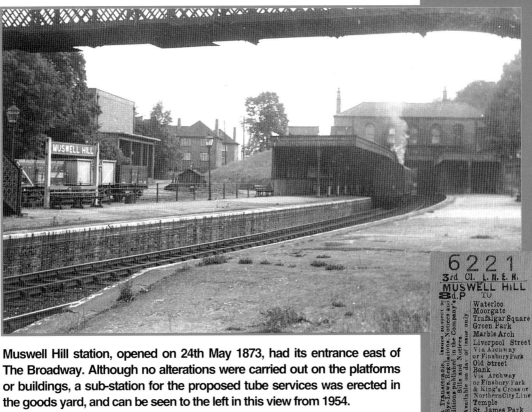

Muswell Hill station, opened on 24th May 1873, had its entrance east of The Broadway. Although no alterations were carried out on the platforms or buildings, a sub-station for the proposed tube services was erected in the goods yard, and can be seen to the left in this view from 1954.

The branch terminus comprised a single island platform for much of its existence, and was totally dwarfed by the huge bulk of Alexandra Palace itself which stood alongside. After closure, the platform was demolished, but the street level building, facing onto The Avenue, still survives and is now used as a community centre.

Express Tube Lines

Following the start of the London Blitz in September 1940, the government decided to build a series of deep level air raid shelters, connected to existing tube stations. These would be constructed by the LPTB on behalf of the Ministry of Home Security, on the understanding that when hostilities ceased they could be linked by new tunnels and used to form express tube lines, which had been proposed in the late 1930s.

A number of sites were considered, but eventually the choice fell on St. Paul's, Chancery Lane, Belsize Park, Camden Town, Goodge Street, Oval, Stockwell, Clapham North, Clapham Common and Clapham South. In all instances the shelters would be positioned either parallel to or below existing station tunnels, and comprise a pair of tubes, each with an internal diameter of 16ft 6ins. These would have a length of 1,400ft, and be lined partly with precast concrete and partly with cast iron. Two floors were to be provided in each tunnel, and these would have enough bunks to accommodate 8,000 people, although the initial number was proposed as 9,600.

The scheme was bugged with labour shortages, and the shelter at Oval was abandoned in 1941, after just 250ft of tunnel, plus a few passageways had been built. A little earlier, the authorities responsible for St. Paul's Cathedral objected to tunnelling being undertaken in their immediate vicinity, so work at St. Paul's was halted, and not resumed.

There was progress elsewhere however, and towards the end of 1942, part of the shelter at Goodge Street was fitted out as headquarters for General Eisenhower. The others were also adapted to serve government needs, and it was not until the onset of Hitler's 'V' weapons, that any were opened for public use. The first was at Stockwell on 9th July 1944, and this was followed by Clapham North (13.7.44.), Camden Town (16.7.44.), Clapham South (19.7.44.) and Belsize Park (23.7.44.). The remainder continued to serve government purposes.

After the war, the shelters were adapted to provide overnight accommodation for soldiers on leave, and other large transient groups, as well as being used for document storage. Goodge Street served as an army transit camp until its closure was hastened by a serious fire in the mid-1950s. At around the same time it was revealed that only the four south London shelters retained the option for conversion to railway use, and the scheme faded into history. In the 1980s, some of the premises were leased as secure archives, with that at Goodge Street being commissioned as 'The Eisenhower Centre' in June 1986. Late in the following decade, the wheel turned almost full circle, when a number of the former deep level shelters were acquired by LT in association with up-grading existing facilities on the Northern Line.

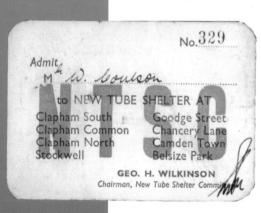

No.329

Admit,
M͚ W. Coulson

to NEW TUBE SHELTER AT

Clapham South   Goodge Street
Clapham Common   Chancery Lane
Clapham North   Camden Town
Stockwell   Belsize Park

GEO. H. WILKINSON
Chairman, New Tube Shelter Committee

This Pass is for use by persons requiring to enter the shelters in the course of their duty and does not authorise the holder to occupy a bunk in the shelter.

Signature of Holder W. Coulson
(C46250)